S0-DZF-358

A HEART FOR GOD
IN INDIA

ARLETA RICHARDSON

A Free Methodist missions publication produced by
the Department of Christian Education,
the Department of World Missions, and the
Women's Missionary Fellowship International

Peggy Payne, Executive Editor
Tamra Yoder, Managing Editor
Jennifer Ortega, Illustrator

ISBN 0-89367-144-4

Table of Contents

Preface

This is the story of the first Free Methodist missionary family in India. Although the church had not yet begun a mission work in that country, the Wards went in faith. They believed that God had called them to work with the Indian people. Their daughters, Ethel, Bessie, and Mary Louise, grew up with a heart of love for India and its people.

I'm indebted to Ethel Ward for the information about her parents in her book called *Ordered Steps*. In it she said, "To the Missionaries' children whose paths have often led to sadness through separations, yet thank God for their rich heritage, and for the privilege of following in their parents' foot-steps."

I would like to dedicate this book to all the missionaries' children today who help their parents with the important work of missions without complaining. May they grow to have a heart for God and a desire to follow His will.

Notes to the Reader

Arleta Richardson, author of the *Grandma's Attic* series, wrote this exciting story about the Ward family, the first Free Methodist missionaries in India. Though the dialog is fiction, it is based on actual situations, people, and conditions in India at the turn of the century. (Throughout the book, Phebe Ward is called Libby, her nickname.)

As you read, catch the thrill of being a young missionary. And remember, you don't need to wait until you're older to be a missionary. You can be one right now! Jesus can use you today to tell others about Him.

Pray for people in the world who don't know Jesus. There are many who need to hear about His love. Jesus asks us to show His love to others wherever we are. So even if you are a kid in the Philippines, Egypt, India, or America, help spread the great news that Jesus loves the world!

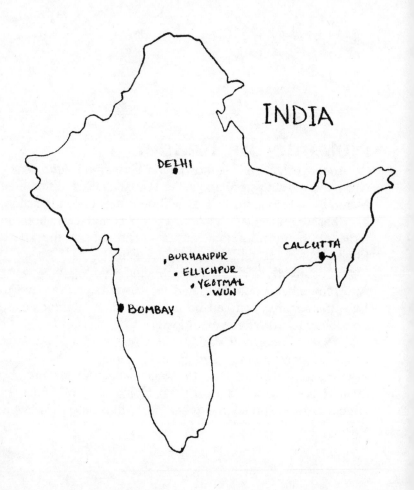

Chapter 1
The Man with the Friendly Smile

"Oh, it's hot!" Libby complained. She plopped down on a chair in front of her tent. "Why does the worst heat of the summer come during camp meeting time?"

"Probably because camp meeting comes during the hottest part of the summer," her friend Polly suggested. "Why are you running around when it's so hot?"

"I haven't been running around." Libby waved a fan in front of her face as she talked. She pushed her damp hair back from her forehead. "I was in the tabernacle listening to the business meetings. My, that place is like the inside of an oven!"

"I didn't know you were interested in the business meetings," Polly remarked. "What are they doing that's so exciting?"

"Nothing," Libby admitted with a grin.

"Nothing? Then why go?" Polly questioned.

"It's not the business that concerns me at all. I really went to see a certain young man. He has such a friendly smile. His name is Ernest Ward."

"He must be something special to risk a heat stroke for," Polly teased. "What does he do for a living?"

"Works in his father's office, I hear." Libby's eyes sparkled as she spoke. "He attended a commercial college in Chicago. He has a good job for a young man. He'll probably take over the family business when his father retires."

"That sounds great, Libby! So when are you getting married?" Polly smirked.

"Married?" Libby exclaimed. "I haven't even met him yet!"

"Unless I'm mistaken, you are about to meet him now. Isn't that Ernest coming this way?"

It was Ernest. He was heading straight for Libby's tent.

Polly disappeared in a hurry, leaving Libby to deal with the young man.

"Good afternoon," he said. "Isn't your name Libby Cox?"

"Yes," she responded.

"My friend tells me you are a schoolteacher. Is that right?" Ernest asked.

Libby swallowed hard. "Yes, I am. Do you need one?" she blurted, then blushed a bright red.

"No," he laughed. "However, I needed to know something about you before I came to speak to you. May I sit down?"

"Of course," Libby replied. "Please do."

After a few minutes of conversation, Ernest asked, "Are you interested in missions?"

"Oh, yes! I've been quite interested in the mission the church just opened in Chicago," Libby commented.

"I know of that mission," Ernest said. "It is doing a great work. But are you interested in foreign missions — going to another country?"

"Foreign missions? I'm afraid I don't know much about that," Libby admitted.

"Then perhaps you should read something about foreign missions," Ernest suggested. "A friend of mine has been a missionary in India for several years. He would like other young people to go there to tell Indians about Christ."

Ernest handed Libby several leaflets about India. "Thank you," Libby responded. "I'm sure I'll enjoy reading these."

After camp meeting closed, Libby returned to her home. She had a new interest in missions and a new ambition.

"Maybe I can save some money from my teaching. I could help pay Ernest's fare to India if that's where the Lord wants him to go," Libby told Polly. "Although India is far away."

"It certainly is far," Polly agreed. "I can't believe you'd meet the man of your dreams, then pay to ship him to the other side of the world!"

But the Lord had other plans for Libby and Ernest. After

a lot of prayer and correspondence, Ernest asked Libby to marry him. He was excited about the way the Lord could use them on the mission field. He wrote, "The Word says 'One shall chase a thousand, and two put ten thousand to flight,' so by merging our steps, our usefulness will be increased tenfold. I believe we can trust God to give us the means to support us."

There was much excitement in the Cox home one October morning in 1880. Forty people were present to celebrate the wedding of Libby Cox and Ernest Ward. They would start their life together by taking the long journey to India.

"What will you need over there in India?" Libby's friends asked her. "What shall we give you for a wedding present?"

"I don't know," Libby replied. "I know we can't take furniture and household goods with us. I don't even know what kind of house we will live in."

Libby soon discovered a lot about India. Even if she had known before leaving what the conditions would be, it would not have changed her mind. Libby was sure that God wanted her to work in India with her new husband.

The Wards planned to take only one small trunk and a suitcase.

"Jesus did say 'Carry neither purse nor scrip,' " Polly observed. "You seem to be obeying that!"

"He also said 'neither shoes'. But we have those," Libby replied with a giggle. "We may not even need them in a hot country like India."

The snow was falling fast on the cold, November day that Libby and Ernest said goodbye. Families and friends watched them board the train for New York. They sailed on the ship named *Anchoria*. After ten days of crossing the Atlantic Ocean, they were delighted to land in Glasgow, Scotland.

"The scenery here is beautiful," Libby wrote home. "Anything looks better than water right now. We will spend a few days in London, then begin the long trip to India. The

12

ship will take us through the British Channel, Bay of Biscay, Straits of Gibraltar, Mediterranean Sea, Red Sea, and Indian Ocean. We look forward to seeing the Suez Canal, but most of all, land again!"

13

Chapter 2
Home in a Strange Land

On January 16, 1881, Libby and Ernest Ward had their first glimpse of India. They arrived at Prince's Dock in Bombay. Missionary friends met the couple and accompanied them to their home in a *gari* (GAH-ree — a two-wheeled horse carriage). After being cramped in a tiny ship's cabin for many weeks, it was wonderful to be in a home.

"We are enjoying the sights and sounds of a strange country," Libby wrote to her family. "We have visited some mission schools and met many missionaries. We will leave soon for Ellichpur, where our work will begin. Can you believe that we are 11,313 miles from our home in Illinois?"

Shortly after arriving in Ellichpur, Libby stood by the door of her bungalow home, which they shared with other missionaries. One of the missionaries was Emma.

"Emma, come quickly!" she called. "You must see what is going by! What in the world is it?"

Emma hurried to the door. "A wedding procession," she said. "Hm, those people must have money."

"How can you tell?" Libby asked. "And where are the bride and groom?"

"I can tell they're wealthy because they have a band and horses. The groom is the little boy being carried on the shoulders of the men. Watch and you will see the bride in a red-covered coach drawn by young bulls."

The coach went by, followed by twenty-four other carts. Libby gazed at the scene in amazement.

"But they are only children!" she exclaimed. "Are you sure this is a wedding and they are the ones getting married?"

"Yes, indeed," Emma said. "The parents choose whom the children will marry. Once the decision is made, there is no changing it. Children are married very young; then the girl goes to live with her mother-in-law. The girl is taught how to keep house and cook. She learns how to be a good wife."

Libby shook her head as the procession moved out of sight. "I'd rather decide for myself whom to marry. I'd want to marry someone that I knew and liked!"

Emma laughed as they walked back into the house. "You will see much in India that seems strange to you," she said. "But the people here have the same need as people everywhere — to know that Jesus can save them from their sins. That's why we have come."

Libby learned many things from Emma before she moved out of the bungalow home. One of the most surprising was that she would be expected to have servants.

"Servants?" she exclaimed. "Why would I need them? I've always taken care of my own housework. And I certainly can cook."

"There are many things you don't understand about India," Emma replied. "You must have a *Munshi* (MOON-shee), a language teacher, if you want to speak with the people. You'll also need a person to wash your laundry. Then you must have a cook who can shop for food. The cook won't carry water though. You'll surely need water for washing and drinking. So you'll need someone to haul water to the home. You see, each person does only his own job."

"And what do I do?" Libby inquired. "With all those people around, I'll be in the way!"

"You have come to tell people about Christ," Emma reminded her. "Your first job will be to learn the language. You also need to acquaint yourself with Indian customs. That will keep you busy."

Libby soon found that this was so. Learning about India was a full-time job.

The mission work took the Wards to Burhanpur, a city of 34,000 people with no gospel workers. Here, they would set up housekeeping on their own.

"We've been promised a house to live in," Ernest told

16

Ernest Ward

Phebe (Libby) Ward

17

Libby. "I'm sure we'll have to take everything with us that we'll need to furnish it."

"Our friends have given us enough to get started," Libby replied. "We should get along with these things."

They began to pack. When they were ready to leave, all their earthly belongings took up very little space. They had a lamp, a table, a pitcher, a pillow, two spoons, two soup bowls, four boxes of matches, a frying pan, tongs, two beds, two chairs, four plates, two glasses, a tea cup, and a tin wash basin.

Libby looked over the collection and laughed. "If Polly thought we left America with little, she should see what we have to furnish our first home. Truly our treasure is in heaven, like the Bible says; it certainly isn't here on earth!"

Everything was loaded. Libby and Ernest traveled forty miles by train to their new location. Two small ox carts carried them the last three miles to the new home which had been promised to them.

When the carts stopped, Libby was thankful to step on the ground again. "I don't think I've ever ridden on anything that rough. Are you sure that's a road?" she teased. "Well, I'm certainly glad to be here!"

However, a few moments later, Libby was ready to get back in the ox cart and return to the train.

"Ernest, where's the house?" she asked. They looked around and were puzzled. Nothing could be seen but a wall stretching along the river which ran by the city.

"Are you sure this is the place?" Ernest asked the men who had brought them. "Is this where we are to live?"

The men nodded. One of them pointed to an opening in the wall. Libby walked over and looked in. Their "house" was one room. There were no windows or doors. There weren't even frames for any! Libby's heart sank. She surveyed the broken walls and the dirt floor. *How can I ever live in a place like this?* she thought.

Ernest stood behind her and looked at the room that was to be their home. He had never seen anything like it.

"Well," Libby said finally, "the floor has been swept. So

it's not too bad."

They moved their things into the room and prepared to make the best of it.

"Thank the Lord! We have some bread and condensed milk left from our lunch," Libby said. She wanted to look on the positive side. "We won't go to bed hungry."

The next morning they found that the open fireplace on the floor was the stove to cook their food. Libby boiled some whole wheat for porridge. The last of the condensed milk was used.

"We can't go on like this," Ernest said. "We must have someone who can shop and buy food for us. We'll pray that the Lord will send someone."

Their prayer was answered that very day. Three men appeared at their door. One took some wheat to grind into flour. Another promised to carry water. The third, who could speak English, promised to be their cook.

This was a shaky beginning for the young missionaries. But in spite of all the new circumstances, they never doubted that God had called them to work in India.

Chapter 3
Working Hard

"We have moved into the city!" Libby wrote happily to her family later that year. "We now have two rooms and a door. Of course the walls and floor are mud, and there are still no windows, but everything has been whitewashed to make it sanitary. We are in the middle of the city, so Ernest is able to be with the people. He is doing very well in learning to talk to them and giving them literature."

Libby was also studying the language with the *Munshi* who came two hours a day. In four weeks, she had learned 615 words in Hindustani. She was quite pleased to be able to talk with the people who lived near them. They soon began to have "family prayers" with those who gathered to hear Bible stories.

One evening Libby was unusually quiet as she and Ernest ate supper.

"Have you had a hard day today, Libby?" Ernest inquired.

"You could say that," she responded. "I made a terrible mistake while trying to tell our neighbor Sashi about my niece in America."

"It couldn't have been that bad," Ernest consoled her. "What did you say?"

"I told her that the baby was nine months old and weighed eleven pounds. But I used the wrong word. Instead of saying the baby weighed eleven pounds, I said the baby had eleven heads!"

Ernest tried hard not to laugh, but he couldn't help it. Soon Libby was laughing with him as they thought about how amazing that news must have sounded to Sashi.

Of course, that was not the last mistake Libby would make trying to speak the new language. One morning she asked an Indian helper to gather all the children together for Sunday school. At least that's what she thought she had asked. However, she discovered her mistake when she found not a yard full of children, but squawking chickens! It was a difference of only one letter in the words. But one letter can make a big difference!

"Even with the silly errors I made," Libby wrote home, "I get along better with the language than I do managing the servants. I knew about the Indian caste system before I came, but I didn't realize what problems I would have in my home. Castes are separate and fixed classes of society. One is born into a caste and must obey the rules. Most of the rules seem to have to do with eating and drinking. No one will eat our food after it is cooked, nor drink water that is stored in the earthen jars we use. One servant will not eat food mixed with water, but will eat fruit we hand to him. Another man will water the garden and bring water for washing and bathing, but not for drinking.

"You would be interested to see how our laundry is done. The man who washes our clothes pounds them with rocks in the river. I soon found out that I had better take the buttons off the shirts and dresses before he got hold of them, or I'd have to replace the whole set every time he washed. Sashi finally came to my rescue. She showed me where to get Indian buttons made with thread. That solved one problem very nicely!"

The Wards soon adjusted to the Indian ways and the Indian people. As they learned to speak the language more easily, Ernest began to travel to surrounding areas to preach. He handed out books. The Indian people were curious about why the Wards had come to India.

"Was there not enough work in your country for you?" they asked.

"There was enough work," Ernest replied. "But we wanted to share the good news of Jesus Christ with you."

Many Indians felt that India didn't need any new religions. However, Ernest continued to hold street meetings. There were always those who wanted to see Americans to hear about their *guru* (GOO-roo — religious leader) Jesus. Ernest carefully explained that Jesus was the Son of the

living God who had died to save everyone.

Ernest's trips were not without danger. Often when traveling by ox cart, he and the Indian workers met tigers and bears at night. When a bear stood in the road, the men would yell. They would beat on tin cans and pull the bells around the oxen's necks. Finally, the bear would decide to let the noisy crowd go by and would move off into the quiet jungle. Ernest soon became brave enough to walk from village to village. Sometimes he walked alone, but often he had an Indian helper.

One day he became separated from his companion. For hours he wandered through the jungle, looking for a village. After a long time, he came into a clearing and fell in front of an Indian home. He was too weak to speak. The man in the home saw Ernest and knew he needed water. Soon Ernest was drinking from the brass *lota* (LOH-tah) the man offered him. Only after he had received a bit did Ernest notice that the kind Indian was covered with smallpox.

"I immediately remembered what the Bible says in Mark 16:18," Ernest told Libby when he returned home. "It says, 'If they drink any deadly thing, it shall not hurt them.' I certainly would not drink something like that on purpose to find out if it's meant for us today. But I trusted God for that promise when I did it without knowing."

The promise was true, all right. Ernest didn't catch smallpox after that experience.

Very soon the rainy season began.

I thought I knew what rain was, Libby remembered as she stood in the doorway and peered out toward the river. *My, but I've never seen it come down like this! Our rain barrel is already running over.*

Later they learned that sixteen inches of rain had fallen in one day! They also found that the greatest danger of the rainy season was the deadly disease called cholera. Many Indians died. The Wards were saddened as they watched the families care for the sick and bury their dead.

"If only they knew the hope of being a Christian," Ernest said. "We must work harder to make sure the Indian

24

people have a chance to meet Jesus. Libby, I know that's why God has sent us to this great land.''

Chapter 4
A New Home

The months went by quickly for Ernest and Libby. It seemed as if they had been in India for just a short time. Yet, nearly two years had passed.

Libby enjoyed visiting with the wives of the Indian gentlemen in the village. Because of the law, these ladies seldom left home. The law said that a woman of social position shouldn't appear in a crowd. The law also said that no man outside her family should see her face. When the wife of a gentleman did leave her house, she covered her head with a veil. Because these women weren't free to meet other people outside their homes, they were happy to have Libby visit.

Libby would read the Bible and pray with them. She also worked with the children.

"Because we don't have a church building, I'll have Sunday school in our yard," she told Ernest. "There are many children in this neighborhood who would love to hear Bible stories. I'll have my helpers invite them to come on Sunday at nine o'clock."

The first Sunday came. Libby eagerly waited for the children to arrive. By nine o'clock there were about fifteen children in the yard.

When Ernest returned from his preaching trip, Libby told him what had happened. "I began to teach the children some choruses. Then I told them a story," she said. "We had just about finished when another dozen children came. So I started all over again. Can you believe this went on all morning! Finally, Sashi told me what the problem was. 'These children don't have clocks,' she said. 'They don't know whether it's nine o'clock or two. You'll have to set the time around something they all do during the day. Then they will be able to come at one time.' I tried that," Libby continued, "and it worked. The next Sunday we had almost

fifty children here for Sunday school!"

"Libby, that's wonderful!" Ernest congratulated her. "I'm sure these children go home and tell the stories to their families, too."

Though the Wards were thankful for a place to stay, they knew they needed a larger place to run the mission. They began to pray that God would direct them to a permanent place to live. At last they were able to buy seven acres of land outside the city gate for 500 *rupees* (ROO-peese). (A *rupee* was about thirty-three cents in American money. So the land cost about $165.) The mango trees on the property had to be bought separately from the land. That was fine — they were worth it for the fruit and shade they gave.

Ernest drew the plans for a house. It was to be square with four large rooms. High walls would help keep the new home cool. There were also smaller rooms for a bathroom and pantry. A porch would surround the entire house. The Wards looked forward to the completion of their new home.

Although they had planned carefully, the money seemed to go faster than they had expected. Soon the Wards were ninety *rupees* in debt. "We'll have to stop work on the house until we have more money," Ernest said one evening. "We can't live on money we don't have."

They were both disappointed. "Lord, help us know how we can take care of this problem," the couple prayed. The next time they received mail, money from an uncle let them continue building the house!

When Christmas arrived that year, Libby and Ernest found they had just two cents to spend for the holiday. "We can be happy without gifts," Libby said. "After all, we have the greatest gift of all — Jesus!"

"You're right, Libby," Ernest agreed. "We can look forward to our finished home. We can also look forward to telling more Indian friends about Jesus. We shouldn't be sad at all."

And they weren't sad that Christmas. Their Indian friends sent gifts of cake, fruit, and flowers. Soon after that, the Wards were able to move into the house. They would live in the house while they continued to finish the inside.

"Today I finished the shelves and put the books and clothes away," Libby wrote to her family. "The white ants are already working on the books and have eaten up several shoes, but I am learning to take joyfully the spoiling of my goods for Jesus' sake."

One day soon after they moved in, a fellow missionary came to visit. He had just returned from America and brought them a box. Friends and relatives had sent them gifts. They unpacked it with joy.

"Oh look!" Libby exclaimed. "Here is some dried fruit and canned goods! We haven't seen some of these things since we left home."

"And here is cloth to make clothes and some tools for me to use," Ernest said. "They didn't forget anything, did they?"

Libby continued to unwrap the gifts. At the bottom of the box was a package full of baby clothes. Libby took them out and looked them over carefully. She was pleased to have them! In just a few months, there would be a little one to wear those small things.

"Look, Ernest!" Libby said. "I didn't know where we would find the money to buy baby things, and here they are!"

"You know, Libby, the Lord has been good to us," Ernest remarked. "He always knows the right time to do everything."

Soon after moving into their new home, the Wards became acquainted with their new neighborhood. They were anxious to make friends with people. The couple wanted to live like the Indians as much as possible. Libby wore a sari (SAH-ree), a dress like the Indian women wore. The sari was a length of cloth with beautiful colors. It was wrapped around the waist for a skirt, then put over one shoulder. Finally, the end was tucked into the waistband. It was a cool dress for the hot weather in India.

Ernest wore a *dhoti* (DHOH-tee), the same type of

clothes Indian gentlemen wore. The *dhoti* was a white cotton suit with a tunic collar. Like the *sari*, the *dhoti* was comfortable in the heat of India.

"Dressing like the people here is a simple thing," Ernest said. "However, I hope it shows our Indian friends that we want to be one with them."

Chapter 5
The Ward Family Grows

Ernest and Libby had planned to have an English nurse present when the baby arrived. However, before the nurse could get there, the baby came. It was a good thing Indian friends were around to help out.

"Oh, dear! What a disappointment!" one of the Indian women said. "It's only a girl!"

The proud mother and father didn't feel that way at all. They were happy to have a healthy daughter. Ethel Ellen was the chosen name for the new baby. The people in the village treated Ethel with love and kindness. As she grew, she learned to speak two languages: English and the Indian language.

Often Ernest was called away to other missions to help in the worship services or to distribute materials. Libby would be lonely while he was gone, but Ethel was a great comfort for her.

One summer the family decided to vacation at a small mountain resort. The camp was high up a mountain.

"We'll live in a tent right among the trees," Ernest told Libby. "There are many English soldiers camped there. I'm sure we'll have an opportunity to tell them about Jesus."

The soldiers were glad to have the Wards there. The men attended the church meetings the missionaries held. It was a great time of sharing.

When they weren't busy with the soldiers, the Wards liked to wander through the woods and discover caves and old forts. One cave was especially interesting. It had large pillars in front and five rooms cut in solid rock. Inside they found a most unusual sight. When worshipers came to the cave with a request to their gods, they would dip their hands in red paint. Then they would slap their hands on the temple walls with their fingers pointing upward. If they thought their prayers were answered, they would return to

the cave. This time they would slap their red-painted hands on the same spot but with the fingers pointed downward.

"Most of the fingers are pointing up," Libby remarked. "Aren't you glad we pray to a God who can answer when we call?"

"Yes, I am," Ernest replied. "And this makes me more anxious to tell the people about a God who loves them and cares about their needs."

The Wards knew God was interested in their needs. Though they didn't receive financial support regularly, the Lord always provided for them. They were especially happy to be able to baptize the first convert, a man named Trimbuck. Trimbuck was a great help to Ernest. They traveled together many miles from village to village, preaching about Jesus. A cart and two bullocks that Ernest managed to buy made the traveling much easier.

"We've been able to reach all kinds of people," Ernest said one day. "We have friends among the English, the Hindus, and the Mohammedans. The Lord is surely working here. We can definitely see a difference in people like Juman."

"Yes," Libby agreed. "Juman's wife has told me that her husband wants to be baptized. I think she will become a Christian, too. She sees the great changes that God has made in her husband."

Soon the day came for Juman's baptism. His family and a group of Christians gathered on the riverbank. As Ernest and Juman stood in the river, Juman decided to say something. "I don't want to be the same old person after I am baptized. I want to have a new name."

"What would you like it to be?" Ernest asked him.

"I will be called Job Ward," Juman replied. "People will know that I have truly changed since I decided to serve the living God."

It wasn't long before Juman's wife and children became Christians. They, too, were baptized and took the name Ward.

"There will be Wards in India many years after we're

35

gone," Libby laughed. "We didn't know we would have such a large family when we came here."

There was a lot of work to be done, but the Wards didn't have much money to use. They were determined never to be in debt. One time when there wasn't much money, the Wards had to sell four new towels, their cart, and small bulls to pay their bills.

"Everything is paid," Ernest said. "We have seven cents left over. It's been several weeks since we've heard from home. Do you think they've forgotten us, Libby?"

"Oh, no!" Libby exclaimed. "The mail is quite slow. Don't worry! We'll hear from them soon. The Lord is going to take care of us, I know."

Libby's great faith was rewarded, for soon they received $500 from a fellow missionary.

"I'm glad it didn't come before," Libby said. "It shows me that the Lord knows when our needs will be the greatest."

The Wards were excited about what God was doing in their area. However, they could see there was more work to be done. They wished other missionaries lived closer to them.

"It would be so good to talk with someone who understands what we're doing here," Libby said. "We have no other Americans here to work with, and we're too far away from other missionaries to visit them."

But like the other times of need, the Lord heard them. Ernest told Libby some good news. "There's a church convention in Secunderabad. I believe we'll be able to attend it!"

The Wards were thrilled about their trip. The convention was just what they needed to help them remember how important their work in India was. They returned home from Secunderabad, praying that the Lord would send them helpers from America.

Chapter 6
A New Missionary

Libby sighed as she folded the letter that had just come from home. It was from friends who had been interested in coming to work with them in India.

"They aren't going to be able to come," Libby said to Ernest. There was disappointment in her voice. "Do you think the Lord has forgotten how much we need help?"

"No, I'm sure He hasn't," Ernest replied. "He has just the right people for us. And He will bring them at just the right time. We must be patient and wait upon the Lord."

Finally, after five long years of praying, new missionaries came to assist the Wards. It was a time of rejoicing.

"We must decorate the house, Ernest. Let's prepare a big welcome dinner for them," Libby said. "I can't believe that they will really be here. We've been praying for this to happen for several years."

Everyone worked hard to get things in order. On February 5, 1886, Louisa Ranf and Julia Zimmerman arrived. The Wards had hung a message saying "Welcome to India." The two ladies knew that they had come to a place where everyone was glad to see them.

Even though they couldn't understand the Indian language yet, Louisa and Julia went with the Wards to visit homes. Helping in Sunday school was another job the two women did. They handed out picture cards to the children.

Shortly after the ladies arrived in India, Ernest received a letter. It was from the missionaries in Ellichpur, the town where the Wards had begun their work.

"We're going back to our mission," the letter said. "You had better return to Ellichpur, because there is no other missionary here."

Return to Ellichpur? Ernest thought. *Why now? We finally have a home here and some help with the work.*

It was hard for them to leave their home in Burhanpur,

but it seemed that the Lord wanted them to go back. They sold their home to another mission and moved into a home near the river in Ellichpur.

"This certainly looks different than the hole in the wall we lived in when we first came!" Libby said when they had moved in. "We have room here for new missionaries and any visitors who come. There are many more rooms."

The big porch was a perfect place for Sunday school. On Sunday morning, there was Sunday school for the English children who lived nearby. In the afternoon, there was a Hindustani Sunday school. The Wards weren't lonely at all. Many people lived and worked in Ellichpur. They also knew there would soon be another child in the Ward family. It was a happy day when a girl, whom they named Bessie, was born.

"What?" said their Indian friends. "Another girl? How unfortunate you are to have only girls in your family. Why has God not blessed you with a boy?"

"We feel that God has blessed us with a girl," Libby told them. "Girls are just as precious as boys in our family."

Older sister Ethel was happy, too. Now that Ethel was seven years old, she was able to entertain the new baby. This allowed the adults to continue working for the mission.

Soon after the Wards moved, one of the helpers, Julia, left India. However, Louisa stayed and helped Libby each day. She was like another member of the missionary family.

"We have had a busy day today," she said one evening at supper. "Libby and I went calling. In one home, we had to take our shoes off before going upstairs. We've never had to do that before."

"Yes," Libby chuckled. "We don't know why we had to do it this time. The floor of the house was no cleaner than the street outside. But we had a good time telling the people about Jesus and praying with them. When we left, a man met us at the door and wanted us to come to his house next."

Louisa picked up the story from there. "We went to his house and had a good time. Everyone seemed interested in

what we had to say. In fact, as we were leaving they invited us to come back often. 'This house is yours,' they said."

One morning Ernest said to Libby and Louisa, "I'm going to walk to the village of Borda today. It's seven miles away, but come with me if you like."

Both ladies wanted to go. While in Borda, Ernest had a chance to preach to an audience. Everyone seemed interested in what he had to say.

When the meeting was over, an old man approached Ernest. "Look! See these?" The man held two little New Testaments that he had purchased from Ernest. "We bought these from you long ago," he said. "We read them all the time."

The Wards were thrilled to see the well-worn pages of the Bibles. Many times they had prayed that lives would be changed because of the materials they gave to others.

When Ernest and Libby's wedding anniversary came that year, Louisa was given some money to plan a special dinner as a celebration.

As the time drew near, Libby called the family together. "I have been thinking about the celebration dinner. It would be nice to have it, but many of our neighbors are so poor. They can't afford even a small meal. I don't think I could enjoy a big dinner when they are in need."

The rest of the family agreed. Instead, they spent that special day helping the people in the village. Doing the Lord's work is what they enjoyed more than anything.

Later that year, the Ward family suffered much sadness. Louisa was accidentally burned when a kerosene lamp fell on her. She died that night and was buried in Ellichpur. The Indian people missed her a lot. She had won their hearts and had shown them Christ's love. Libby was upset at losing a good friend. But because Louisa knew Jesus as her Savior, Libby knew that Louisa was with the Lord.

Chapter 7
Home to America!

When news of Louisa's death reached America, many of her dear friends talked about who would go to India to take her place. A young lady by the name of Celia Ferries was working for the Free Methodist Church in Chicago when the news came.

"I'll go to India," she said. "If it's the Lord's will for me, I'll certainly go."

She soon realized that God did want her to help in India. Many sacrifices were made by others so Celia could join the Wards.

"How good the Lord is to send Celia!" Libby exclaimed when the news reached them. "It'll be like welcoming a relative because we know her family in Illinois."

A place was made for the new missionary in the Ward family. Celia was greeted with roses and kisses.

The next six weeks were spent in Chikalda, the nearest cool place to Ellichpur. While they were there, Ernest preached one evening. Ethel told her mother that she wanted to be saved like her parents. Gladly, Libby prayed with her little daughter. They prayed that Jesus would forgive Ethel for all the things she had done that displeased Him. After her prayer, Ethel wanted to testify about what Jesus had done for her. It was an exciting time for the Ward family.

Four months after Celia Ferries arrived, they found a good teacher in the Marathi language. She at once began to study, and the Wards began to think of a trip back to America. It would be their first time to go home since they had come to India. That had been almost ten years ago!

Ethel was overjoyed at the thought of the trip. Libby had been giving her daily lessons in reading, writing, and arithmetic.

Libby encouraged Ethel to study hard. "You'll have to

know more English if you go to America. You'll want them to understand you."

"I'll work hard to learn English," Ethel promised. "I do want to see America where my grandparents and uncles and aunts and cousins live. And we will see snow, right?"

"Yes, Ethel," her mother assured her. "You will see snow and many other wonderful things."

Many, many times that year Ethel asked her parents when the family would go to America. It seemed like such a long wait for a young girl.

So much had to be done before they could leave. First of all, they needed to have money for the long trip.

Ernest came home one day with happy news. "Missionaries have come from England. They want to begin work here in Ellichpur, and they offered to buy our home."

"That is definitely an answer to prayer," Libby replied. "It's a relief to know that someone will be telling the people in Ellichpur about Jesus even though we'll be away."

The day to leave for America finally came! The Wards had to travel to the city of Bombay to catch the ship for the long voyage. While the Wards were in Bombay, they had the pleasure of meeting two young missionaries who had just arrived from America. The young missionaries, Miss Douglas and Miss Sherman, were eager to start work in India. So the Wards helped them organize a church in Byculla. It began with seven English-speaking people from the city.

Finally, all arrangements were made for sailing. The family said goodbye to their adopted land of India.

Ethel and Bessie ran about the ship and explored everything they could. Spending many days on the ship didn't bother the girls. They enjoyed every minute. However, every time the ship docked in a city they would ask, "Is this America?"

When the ship finally landed in America, Ernest and Libby were as excited as their daughters. The first glimpse of the Statue of Liberty in New York Harbor brought tears to their eyes. It had been nearly twelve years since they had been home. Things looked quite a bit different to them.

"Mama, are you sure we should ride on the cars that have no horses to pull them?" Ethel asked anxiously.

Libby had never ridden an electric car either. But together the family traveled on this new kind of transportation. Electricity lighted the cities. Other wonders like the telephone were shown to them for the first time.

"What do you like most of all in New York?" Libby asked Ernest when they had been there several days.

Ernest thought electricity was the greatest thing. Libby didn't agree.

"The very best thing is the indoor plumbing," she declared. "Imagine not having to carry water from the river or the well to do all the cooking, bathing, and washing!"

Soon the family was ready to leave New York and travel on to Illinois. The train poked along until they arrived at the station in Cary.

"There they are!" Libby exclaimed. She pointed out the window at her three brothers who had come to meet them.

Those were happy days with loved ones. But Ernest and Libby were anxious to travel to many churches and camp meetings where they were invited to speak on India. Interested people wanted to know more about the work the Wards were doing.

They traveled as far east as Pennsylvania and as far west as California. They dressed in Indian costume, sang Indian songs, and talked about their beloved India. Everywhere they went, Ethel and Bessie saw different and wonderful things. These were things they had only heard about while they lived in India.

That summer the family returned to California. It was here that their last baby girl arrived. This time no one said, "What a shame! It's just another girl!" Instead, their friends rejoiced with them in the coming of the newest member of the family.

"We will name her Mary Louise in memory of our dear Louisa Ranf," Libby said. "God gave these girls to me. I want them to grow up wanting to serve Him like Louisa did."

Chapter 8
The Family Together

Too soon the time came for the Wards to return to India. Although Ernest and Libby were anxious to see their friends in India again, it was difficult to leave America. The hardest part of the return was the decision to leave Ethel and Bessie in America to continue their education.

"We prayed a long time about this," Libby said to Ernest as they prepared to leave. "I'm sure it's the best thing to do. But I can hardly stand the thought of going back without my girls."

"It's hard for me, too," Ernest confessed. "But we know they must have an education. Ethel will look after Bessie. The two of them will comfort each other. There are no schools for missionaries' children in India. You don't have time to teach them at home either."

"I know," Libby replied. "We don't know where we'll be living either. I'm glad that we learned of the children's school and home in Virginia, where they will be cared for."

Libby, Ernest, and baby Louise were ready to leave for India. Meanwhile, Ethel and Bessie joined other children in the school in Virginia. It would be five long years before they would see their parents again.

The Wards arrived back in India. There was a terrible famine taking place in the land. Little food meant that people were going hungry.

"Our Sunday morning meetings are times to distribute grain to the starving people," Libby wrote home. "We have decided to give out one meal a day to those who are the neediest. Parents have brought children and left them with us, and the police bring those who have no parents. Our family of orphans has increased to 664."

When it became impossible for Ernest and Libby to care for them, missionaries came from other places and took children to care for. Some children went to Bombay and

The bungelow at Wun in 1904 was home for the Ward family.

some to Yeotmal. It was hard for Libby to watch these children suffer. However, she was happy to see those they were able to feed become healthy. They would begin to play and sing again.

In 1898, the Wards made plans to return to America. Their greatest joy was to be with Ethel and Bessie again. The girls were overjoyed to see their parents. Like their last trip to America, the Wards visited with family and friends. They also had time to travel and tell other Christians about the hungry orphans in India.

This time when they returned to India, Ethel and Bessie went, too. The whole family was together for the first time since little Mary Louise had been born. Mary Louise didn't know her sisters when they first arrived in the United States. But it didn't take long for her to warm up to them.

At the beginning of the new year, Ernest received a letter from the Yeotmal district in India. The letter said, "Come home. We need you. Four of our missionaries have gone, and we have an empty bungalow house for you to live in."

All five Wards were excited and happy to hear this news! It was the first home that they would have to themselves as a family. They thanked the Lord for the nice house. Then they began to explore it: a front room, two bedrooms, two bathrooms, an office, a pantry, and a large porch.

"Look, Mama!" Ethel called. "Everything is furnished for us. I've found some canned goods and dried fruit in the cupboards."

"And see what I've found?" Louise asked. "An organ! Isn't that great? Maybe we can play duets on it, Bessie."

The organ squeaked and wheezed instead of making beautiful sounds. But the girls enjoyed it anyway. So began some of the happiest years the Ward family spent in India. They studied the Marathi language together. After having lessons at home for awhile, Ethel and Bessie attended a nearby high school for two years.

Libby began to pray that a way would open for Ethel to attend Seattle Seminary in America. Because she was the oldest daughter, it was decided that she would go first. The

The Wards together again in India.

other girls would follow when the time came. Libby's prayer was answered. In 1905, Ethel left India again to continue her schooling in Washington state.

This would not end Ethel's years in India. The country where she had been born was dear to her heart. As an adult, Ethel Ward spent many happy and busy days in the land to which God had called her parents more than twenty-five years before.

The Lord certainly blessed the Ward family for their faithfulness to Him. Though they endured hardships and sadness, they found great joy in bringing the love of God to the people of India.

Glossary and Pronunciation Guide

dhoti (DHOH-tee) — white cotton suit worn with a tunic worn by gentlemen in India

gari (GAH-ree) — a two-wheeled cart drawn by a horse

guru (GOO-roo) — spiritual leader

lota (LOH-tah) — brass or copper drinking vessel

Marathi (mah-RAH-tee) — one of the languages spoken in India

Munshi (MOON-shee) — a language teacher

rupees (ROO-pees) — unit of money in India

sari (SAH-ree) — a long piece of fabric which is wrapped around the waist and brought over the shoulder and worn by women in India

"The Ward Triad" as their father called
them — Ethel, Bessie, and Mary Louise.